STILL WITH YOU:

THE BOND THAT REMAINS AFTER LOSS

By

TONY BELL

Dedication

To my beloved spouse, who stood beside me in grief with courage and grace.

To Dean Michael P. Clancey, Lori Zapata, Dean Mary Schofield and Dean George Castagnola, Jr., whose compassion and generosity during one of the most difficult times in my life will never be forgotten.

And to my mother, for a lifetime of unconditional love.

Table of Contents

PART I: UNDERSTANDING GRIEF

CHAPTER 1:
When Grief Arrives Without Warning

Some losses give us time. Others arrive without warning and split life into *before* and *after*.

This chapter is for the kind of grief that comes suddenly—the kind that does not give you a chance to prepare, to say goodbye, or to slowly adjust to a new reality. The kind that leaves you stunned, disoriented, and questioning how the world could possibly continue moving forward.

I know this kind of grief intimately.

A Loss That Changed Everything

My daughter was born with holes in her heart. From the moment she entered the world, our lives revolved around doctors' appointments, medications, careful monitoring, keeping her fed on her feeding machine 24 hours each day and the quiet fear that lives beneath the surface of every parent caring for a medically fragile child.

For a long time, we lived in vigilance.

Then, one day, the cardiologist told us something we had been hoping to hear: the holes appeared to be closing on their own. Her condition was improving. The medications she had been on were discontinued. We were told she was doing well.

We exhaled.

Six months later, I woke up one morning and went to her bedroom.

I found her lifeless body.

There was no warning.
No illness. No hint that her heart was failing her.
No crisis the night before.

One moment, she was a vibrant hyperactive child full of life, energy and bounce who had been improving. The next, she was gone and I'm desperately doing CPR on her lifeless corpse on the floor of our hallway while waiting for the paramedics to arrive hoping that she would breath and life would return to her body that was there relentlessly void of life.

There are no words that fully capture what that kind of moment does to a person.

Shock doesn't begin to describe it.

When the World Stops Making Sense

Sudden loss dismantles your sense of reality. It doesn't arrive as sadness alone—it traumatically arrives as disorientation.

You question everything:

- How could this happen?
- Why wasn't there a sign?
- What did I miss?
- How does life continue when mine has just been shattered?

For a long time, I moved through the world feeling like I was watching my life from the outside. My routines continued, but nothing felt real. The person I was before that morning no longer existed, and I didn't yet know who I was becoming.

What made it even harder was this: before losing my daughter, I had learned to bottle up my emotions. I had learned the art of how to be strong by staying silent, by pushing feelings down, by moving forward without acknowledging what hurt. After all, "Big boys don't cry."

That approach failed me completely.

Grief does not respond to suppression.
It mercilessly demands to be felt.

Learning How to Grieve

Eventually, I entered grief therapy—not because I wanted to relive the pain, but because I couldn't survive by avoiding it.

Therapy taught me something essential: grief is not something you "get over." It is something you **learn how to carry**.

I learned that emotions don't disappear when ignored—they intensify. Ignoring it doesn't make it go away.

I learned that strength is not the absence of feeling, but the willingness to sit with it.

I learned that love does not end just because a life does.

Some days were unbearable.

Some days, I didn't want to wake up—not because I wanted to leave this world, but because opening my eyes meant remembering what had happened all over again.

If you have felt that way, please know this: it does not mean you are weak. It means your heart has been deeply wounded.

What Grief Can Become

Grief changes you. There is no returning to who you were before.

But there *is* a becoming.

Over time, with support, honesty, and patience, I began to realize something unexpected: this loss, while it would never be something I would choose, was shaping me into someone more compassionate, more present, and more committed to helping others who were walking a similar path.

Pain does not have to be the end of your story.

It can become:

- empathy instead of isolation
- purpose instead of numbness
- connection instead of silence

Not because the loss was "meant to happen," but because *you are still here.*

If This Feels Familiar to You

If you are reading this while carrying a loss that feels unbearable—especially one that came without warning—I want you to know why I am sharing this with you.

I am not sharing it to compare pain.

I am not sharing it to offer easy answers.

I am sharing it because sudden loss can make you feel profoundly alone, and you are not.

If some days feel impossible, that does not mean they always will.

If you feel broken, that does not mean you are beyond healing.

Grief does not mean that love failed.

It means that your love was real.

And if you are still here, still reading, still breathing—you are already doing something courageous.

Moving Forward, Gently

You do not need to rush healing.
You do not need to "be strong" for anyone else.
You do not need to know what comes next.

You only need permission to grieve honestly.

In the chapters ahead, we will talk about ways to carry grief with support, how connection and remembrance can coexist with healing, and how you do not have to walk this alone.

Because if you are going through something similar to what I went through, I want you to know this:

Your life is not over.
Your love still matters.
And your story is not finished.

CHAPTER 2:
Why Love Doesn't Simply Disappear

After a loss, many people find themselves experiencing things they did not expect and do not quite know how to name.

A loved one may suddenly come to mind for no obvious reason.
A dream may feel unusually vivid or emotionally charged.
A wave of emotion may arrive without warning.
At times, there may be a quiet sense of comfort, closeness, or presence that feels difficult to explain.

For some, these moments feel confusing. For others, they feel reassuring. For many, they feel like both at once.

What matters most is this: **these experiences are common, they are human, and they are deeply rooted in love**.

They do not mean that you are imagining things incorrectly.
They do not mean that you are failing to "move on."
And they do not require proof or explanation to be meaningful.

The Mind, the Heart, and Love in Motion

When someone we love dies, the relationship does not simply vanish. What changes is the *form* of the relationship, not the fact that it existed.

The human mind does not erase attachment on command. The heart does not forget connection because a body is no longer present.

Instead, the mind and heart begin the slow work of **integration**.

Integration means learning how to hold love, memory, and loss at the same time. It means allowing what mattered to continue having a place in your inner world, even as your external world changes.

This process can show up as:

- memories surfacing unexpectedly
- emotional responses tied to shared experiences
- dreams that revisit moments of closeness you shared together
- a feeling of being guided by what someone taught you

These are not signs of weakness. They are signs that your love was and is real.

When Thoughts Arrive Without Warning

Many people worry when thoughts of their loved one appear suddenly.

They wonder:

- "Why am I thinking of them right now?"
- "Does this mean I'm not healing?"
- "Am I supposed to still feel this connected?"
- "Is it normal to cry at the drop of a hat?"

The truth is that **love does not operate on a schedule**.

Thoughts often arise because the mind is making connections—linking present moments to past experiences, values, and emotional bonds. A sound, a smell, a phrase, or even a quiet moment can open a door to a cherished memory.

This is not regression.
It is continuity.

Dreams and the Language of Emotion

Dreams after loss can feel especially intense. Some are comforting. Some are painful. Some feel symbolic, while others feel strikingly real.

Dreams are one of the ways the brain processes emotion, memory, and unresolved feeling. When grief is present, dreams often become more vivid because the emotional material being processed is profound.

Rather than asking what a dream *means*, it can be more helpful to ask:

- What did I feel during it?
- What part of my relationship is being acknowledged?
- What emotions might be asking for attention?

Dreams are usually not instructions. They are often expressions.

Emotional Waves and the Body's Memory

Grief does not live only in thoughts—it lives in the body.

Sudden sadness, warmth, longing, or calm can arise without a clear mental trigger because the body remembers connection in its own way. Music, anniversaries, seasons, or moments of quiet can activate emotional memory before the conscious mind catches up.

This can be unsettling if you expect grief to follow certain rules.

But grief does not follow rules.
Grief follows love.

Connection Does Not Always Mean Communication

It is important to say this gently and clearly: **connection does not always mean communication**.

Connection can mean:

- carrying someone's values forward
- making choices influenced by what they taught you
- feeling supported by the love you shared
- allowing memory to shape who you are becoming

Sometimes a connection is active.
Sometimes it is subtle.
Sometimes it is simply the quiet permission to remember without pain overwhelming you.

Allowing love to continue existing does not prevent healing. It *is* part of the healing.

Making Space Without Forcing Meaning

One of the most compassionate things you can do for yourself is to allow these experiences to exist **without forcing an interpretation**.

You do not need to label every feeling or thought.
You do not need to explain them to anyone else.
You do not need to decide what they "mean."

You only need to acknowledge that love leaves an imprint.

And that imprint does not disappear simply because a life has ended.

A Gentle Reframe

Rather than asking, *"Why am I still feeling this?"* You might gently ask, *"How is love learning to live differently now?"*

Grief is not the absence of love. It is love adapting to loss.

In the chapters ahead, we will explore how to create healthy space for remembrance, how community supports this process, and how honoring love forward can bring steadiness and meaning over time.

For now, it is enough to know this:

What you are experiencing is not strange.
It is not wrong.
It is not a failure to heal.
It is your love, continuing in a new form.

Chapter 3: Common Grief Experiences (You Are Not Alone)

Grief rarely arrives as a single emotion.

More often, it comes as a shifting landscape—one feeling rising, another receding, sometimes several existing at once. This can be deeply confusing, especially if you expected grief to follow a predictable path or to soften steadily over time.

Many people in grief quietly wonder if what they are feeling is normal.

It is.

Guilt for What Was Unsaid or Undone

One of the most common emotions after loss is guilt.

Guilt may take many forms:

- guilt over words not spoken
- guilt over conversations postponed
- guilt over moments missed
- guilt over choices made with the information you had at the time

The human mind has a tendency to replay the past in search of a version where the outcome might have been different. This is not because you failed—it is because your heart is trying to understand a loss that feels so impossible to accept.

Guilt often emerges not from wrongdoing, but from our **love colliding with finality**.

It is important to remember this: you made decisions and lived moments within the limits of what you knew and what was possible at the time. Grief does not grant hindsight for comfort—it grants it for questioning.

That does not mean the questions have answers.

For years after the death of my daughter I was plagued with tremendous guilt. Guilt that as her father I should have done something, anything to keep her from dying. Even if there was literally nothing else that I could've done to prevent her death I still felt responsible somehow because how could any loving father not keep his child from the forces of death. After all, my most important job in life was protecting her and keeping her safe. How could I fail at my most important responsibility? For this, guilt plagued me.

If you have been bitten by the rabid fangs of guilt understand that you have to release that. Beyond any reasonable doubt, you need to know that your loved one wants you to release the guilt because it is a poison that hurts you and doesn't bring them physically back.

Anger at Timing, Circumstance, or Fate

Anger is another emotion many people feel ashamed to admit.

You may feel angry at:

- the timing of the loss
- the circumstances surrounding it
- medical systems, accidents, or randomness
- life itself for continuing on
- your Higher Power for allowing this to happen

Anger does not mean you loved less. It often means you loved deeply and feel profoundly wronged by what happened.

Anger can coexist with sadness, longing, and love. It does not cancel them out.

Allowing yourself to acknowledge your anger—without acting destructively on it—is part of honest grief.

As a pastor who had devoted his life to helping others since being a teenager, I was afraid to admit it but I was angry at God. Angry because I helped thousands of others in life in the name of this God, sacrificed my last penny so many times to give to helping people "in the name of this God" and this same God didn't save the life of my daughter when I needed help?

Anger is real. If you feel angry understand that it is alright. It is normal and it is completely acceptable.

Fear of Forgetting

Some people are afraid that healing means forgetting. Some people feel guilty to heal, to allow themselves to laugh or even to "not cry".

They worry that if the pain softens, the connection will fade. They may hold tightly to grief because it feels like proof that love still exists. Somehow if they stop actively grieving they somehow didn't love strong enough or felt what they were "supposed to be feeling".

This fear is understandable.

But memory does not depend on suffering.
Love does not require pain to remain real.

You can remember without being overwhelmed.
You can honor without being consumed.

Healing does not erase connection—it changes how you carry it.

Fear of Remembering Too Much

At the same time, others fear the opposite.

They fear that memories will overwhelm them—that a song, a date, a smell or a place will open a door they cannot close. They may avoid reminders entirely, believing distance is safer than closeness.

This, too, is a protective response.

Grief can feel like standing at the edge of something vast and unpredictable. Avoidance is often the nervous system's attempt to maintain balance. Why? Because the flow of constant tears has an effect on a person who is grieving.

Personally, for months I was afraid to go to the store or in public places for very long because I was afraid of the moments that I would be walking down the aisle of the store. I would see something that reminded me of my daughter and then immediately a flood of tears would turn on like a forceful incessant hydrant. When this would happen it was inevitably while others were nearby seeing me and asking me if I was ok, which would increase the flow even more.

Over time, with support, memories can become less destabilizing and more integrated. They do not have to arrive all at once.

The Pressure to "Move On"

Perhaps one of the most painful aspects of grief comes not from within, but from outside.

People may say:

- "They would want you to be happy."
- "It's time to move on."
- "You have to be strong."

Often these words are offered with good intentions. But they can leave the grieving person feeling misunderstood or rushed.

There is no timeline for grief.

There is no finish line you are expected to cross.

Grief does not end because time passes. It changes because *you* change, slowly and unevenly, as you learn to live with what has happened.

There Is No Correct Emotional Order

Some days you may feel calm.
Other days you may feel shattered.
Sometimes you may even feel moments of joy—and then you feel guilt for feeling the joy.

This does not mean you are regressing.

Grief does not move in stages. It moves in **waves**.

Just like when you are sitting on the beach at the ocean. The tide brings the powerful water and waves pushing them up onto the sand wiping away any little sand castles that were constructed there.

Sometimes the waves are gentle. Sometimes the waves surge with more force and pressure. In the same way, our emotions can go hours where it seems they have settled a little but then a scent, a song or a sound triggers a memory and grief pulls the waves higher like the moon does to the tide of the ocean.

You are not doing it wrong if your emotions arrive stronger or out of order. There is no correct sequence and no required destination.

Grief Is Not Something You Solve

One of the most freeing truths about grief is this:

Grief is not a problem to be solved.

It is not a puzzle with missing pieces.
It is not a task to complete successfully.

Grief is an experience to be integrated.

Integration means:

- allowing emotions to exist without judgment
- letting grief inform you, not define you
- learning how to carry love forward in a changed world

You do not need to rush this process.
You do not need to perform it correctly.
You only need permission to be where you are.

A Gentle Reminder

If you recognize yourself in any of these experiences—guilt, anger, fear, pressure, confusion—please know this:

You are not alone.
You are not failing.
You are grieving.

And grief, as painful as it is, is one of the most human responses to love we have.

In the next chapters, we will explore how support, community, and intentional remembrance can help transform grief from something isolating into something shared and steady.

For now, it is enough to know that what you are feeling makes sense.

And you do not have to carry it alone.

A Gentle Reflection (Optional)

You do not need to complete this exercise "correctly."
You do not need to finish it in one sitting.
You are free to stop at any point.

This is simply an invitation.

Find a quiet moment, even if it is brief. You may want a notebook, or you may prefer to reflect silently. Safely light a remembrance candle.

1. **Name What Is Present Right Now**: Without trying to change anything, notice what you are feeling in this moment. You might name one emotion, several, or none at all.

If words are difficult, that is okay. You might simply notice sensations in your body—tightness, heaviness, warmth, or calm.

There is no need to analyze what you find.

2. **Acknowledge One Common Grief Experience**: Look back at the emotions discussed in this chapter:

- guilt
- anger
- fear of forgetting
- fear of remembering
- pressure to move on

If one stands out to you, gently acknowledge it.

You might say to yourself:

"It makes sense that I feel this way."

You do not need to resolve it.

3. **Offer Yourself a Moment of Compassion**: Imagine speaking to yourself as you would to someone you love who is grieving.

What would you say to them right now?

If words do not come, you might simply place a hand over your heart or take one slow breath.

Compassion does not require answers.

4. **Close the Reflection**: When you are ready, bring the exercise to a close.

You might remind yourself:

"I am allowed to grieve at my own pace."

Or simply return to your day.

CHAPTER 4:
When Someone We Love Dies

When someone we love dies, many people carry a quiet, unspoken question:

Am I allowed to stay connected?

Some worry that staying connected means being unable to heal. Others fear that letting go of pain means letting go of love. Still others feel unsure about what connection is "supposed" to look like after a loss.

It helps to begin with this truth:

Connection does not require rituals, belief systems, or explanations.

Connection is not something you must justify or defend. It is something that continues naturally because love existed.

Connection Is Simple, Not Ceremonial

In grief, people sometimes assume that honoring love must be dramatic, symbolic, or complex. In reality, the healthiest forms of connection are often the simplest and most personal.

Healthy ways to honor your love include:

- speaking your loved one's name
- writing letters, you never send
- lighting a remembrance candle on anniversaries, difficult days or once a week

- sharing stories with others
- allowing emotions without judgment

None of these require spiritual language.
None require public display.
None require belief beyond acknowledging that the relationship mattered.

Connection does not need to be elaborate to be meaningful

Speaking Their Name

Many people stop saying a loved one's name because they fear it will make others uncomfortable, or because they worry it will intensify the pain.

But names carry presence. Names are important.

Saying someone's name does not pull you backward. It acknowledges that they were real, that they mattered, and that their life still holds meaning.

You are allowed to say their name.
You are allowed to let their name remain part of your world.

Writing Letters, You Never Send

Writing is often one of the safest ways to give grief a voice.

Letters you never send may include:

- things you wish you had said
- questions you never had answers to
- gratitude
- frustration or anger
- updates about your life

These letters are not meant to fix anything. They are meant to **give expression to what remains unfinished**.

You do not need to reread them.
You do not need to keep them.

The act of writing itself often brings relief.

Lighting a Candle on Meaningful Days

For many people, lighting a remembrance candle provides a quiet, grounding way to mark time.

A candle can represent:

- remembrance
- continuity
- intention
- acknowledgment

It does not need to be part of a ritual.
It does not need words.

Sometimes it is simply a way to pause and say, *"You mattered, and you still do."*

Sharing Stories With Others

Stories allow love to move outward instead of remaining locked inside.

Sharing stories:

- keeps memory alive
- reduces isolation

- reminds others who your loved one was
- reminds you who you were with them

Stories do not need to be inspiring or complete. Ordinary memories—the small, imperfect and unassuming moments—are often the most healing.

Allowing Emotions Without Judgment

Connection also means allowing yourself to feel without deciding whether the feeling is appropriate or timely.

You may feel sadness and warmth at the same time.
You may feel peace one day and longing the next.
You may feel nothing at all for a while.

There is no correct emotional response.

Allowing emotions to move without judgment gives grief room to soften naturally instead of hardening through resistance.

Ancestral Remembrance Altars: A Physical Space for Connection

For some people, connection feels easier when it has a physical place to rest.

This is where **ancestral remembrance altars** can be helpful—not as a spiritual requirement, but as a **gentle, intentional space for memory**.

An ancestral remembrance altar is simply a small, personal area set aside to honor those who came before you. It is not about summoning, communication, or belief. It is about **acknowledgment and continuity**.

In many cultures and families, this practice has existed for generations. In modern grief care, it is often used as a grounding tool—a way to give love and memory a home.

What an Ancestral Remembrance Altar Looks Like

An altar does not need to be elaborate. It can be as simple as:

- a small table, shelf, or corner
- a candle
- a photograph or written name
- a meaningful object
- a quiet, intentional placement

Some people add:

- flowers or plants
- a cloth
- a small bowl or keepsake

What matters is not what is included, but **why the space exists**.

The altar becomes a place where:

- you can pause
- you can remember
- you can reflect
- you can acknowledge love without urgency

It is not a place you must visit daily.
It is not a place of obligation.

It is simply a space that says: *"You still belong in my story."*

How Altars Support Healing

For many people, remembrance altars help by:

- externalizing grief instead of keeping it contained
- reducing the fear of forgetting
- offering structure during emotionally heavy periods
- creating a sense of steadiness

They allow connection to exist **without clinging**.

You are not holding on—you are making room.

Connection Is Not About Clinging

It is important to say this clearly:

Healthy connection is not about refusing to move forward.

It is not about avoiding life or change.
It is not about staying in pain.

Healthy connection acknowledges that love still has a place—even as life continues.

You are allowed to grow.
You are allowed to experience joy.
You are allowed to build a future.

None of this erases the past.

Love is not diminished by living.

Making Space for What Remains

Connection does not have to be constant.
It does not have to be intense.
It does not have to be visible to anyone else.

Sometimes your connection is simply the quiet understanding that someone helped shape who you are.

That understanding can live gently alongside everything that comes next.

A Gentle Reflection (Optional)

This reflection is an invitation only.
There is no expectation to act immediately.

1. Notice What Form of Connection Feels Safest Right Now
From this chapter, notice what feels most approachable:

- speaking their name
- writing a letter
- lighting a remembrance candle
- sharing a story
- imagining a small remembrance space

You are not choosing a commitment—only noticing what resonates.

2. Imagine a Place for Memory: If you were to create a small space—physical or symbolic—to honor your loved one, what might it look like?

You might imagine:

- where it would be
- what it might include

- how often you might visit it

There is no correct answer.

3. Check in With Your Body: As you imagine this, notice how your body responds.

If there is resistance, that is information—not failure.
If there is calm or warmth, that is information too.

Both are valid.

4. Close With Permission: You might gently remind yourself:

"I am allowed to stay connected in ways that feel healthy for me."

Then return to your day.

Connection does not require effort.
It requires permission.

In the next chapter, we will explore what happens when grief becomes heavy and how support—both personal and communal—can help carry what feels too much to hold alone.

For now, it is enough to know this:

Love does not disappear.
It adapts.
And you are allowed to give it a place to rest.

CHAPTER 5:
When Grief Becomes Heavy

Grief does not remain the same from day to day.

Sometimes it moves like an ocean tide—rising, receding, giving brief moments of rest. At other times, it settles into the body like a weight that does not lift, even when nothing new has happened.

When grief becomes extremely heavy, people often assume they are failing at grief. They believe they should be "coping better", "adjusting faster", or "handling it" more quietly.

But heaviness is not a sign that you are doing something wrong.

Heaviness is a sign that grief has reached a point where **it needs to be shared**.

Grief deserves compassion—and sometimes, it deserves support beyond what one person can provide alone.

The Quiet Shift Into Heaviness

Grief rarely announces when it has crossed from something painful but manageable into something heavier.

The shift is often subtle.

You may still be functioning. You may still be meeting obligations. On the surface, things may look "fine." But internally, something feels more strained, more exhausting, more fragile.

This shift can feel confusing because nothing obvious has changed—yet everything feels harder.

That does not mean you are regressing.
It means grief is asking for a different kind of care.

Signals the Nervous System Sends

The body often recognizes the need for support before the mind does.

Support becomes especially important when:

- sleep disappears or becomes consistently disrupted
- isolation increases and contact with others feels effortful
- guilt becomes constant rather than occasional
- meaning or hope can often feel distant, fragile, or lost

These are not your personal shortcomings.
They are **signals for you**.

Just as physical pain alerts us to injury, emotional pain alerts us to strain. Ignoring those signals does not make grief lighter—it often causes it to deepen and harden.

Sleep Loss and the Cost of Staying Alert

Sleep is one of the first body systems that grief disrupts.

You may lie awake replaying moments.
You may wake too early, already exhausted.
You may sleep for long hours and still feel unrested.

This is not a failure of discipline or routine. It is the nervous system remaining on alert after loss—especially after sudden or traumatic loss.

I remember after my daughter died I didn't want to get out of bed but didn't have a choice because my other kids needed me. At night tears and memories wouldn't allow me to sleep so my body suffered greatly, which of course impacted my emotions and further perpetrated the cycle of mourning.

When sleep disappears for extended periods, grief becomes much harder to process alone. Support helps regulate what grief has unsettled, allowing the body to rest enough for healing to begin.

Isolation and the Shrinking of the World

Grief often narrows life.

Social interactions may feel draining or pointless. Conversations may feel awkward or superficial. You may feel disconnected from people who have not experienced similar loss, even when they mean well.

While some withdrawal is natural, prolonged isolation, unfortunately, can intensify grief's weight.

Humans are not meant to grieve in isolation. Historically and psychologically, grief has always been held in **community**, even when that community is small.

Being witnessed—without being fixed, rushed, or corrected—lightens grief in ways nothing else can.

Guilt That Refuses to Quiet

Guilt is one of grief's most persistent companions.

Some guilt arises from specific moments or decisions. Other guilt has no clear source—it lingers, repeats, and resists reassurance.

Persistent guilt often signals:

- unresolved questions that cannot be answered
- a sense of responsibility for what could not be controlled
- a mind trying to restore order after chaos

This kind of guilt does not respond to logic. It responds to **compassion**, perspective, and often to the presence of someone who can help hold what feels unbearable alone.

When Meaning Begins to Slip Away

Perhaps the most disorienting aspect of heavy grief is the loss of meaning.

You may wonder:

- "What is the point of going on now?"
- "Who am I without them?"
- "How do I live in a world that feels permanently altered since they have gone?"

These questions are not signs of hopelessness. They are signs of **transition**.

Losing a loved one changes the structure of meaning. Support does not replace what was lost—but it helps you discover how meaning can exist again, differently.

The Pressure to Carry It Alone

Many people resist seeking help because they believe they should be able to handle grief independently.

They tell themselves:

- "Others have survived worse."
- "Only weak people get therapy."
- "What will people think?"
- "I don't want to burden anyone."
- "I should be stronger than this."

These beliefs often come from survival strategies learned long before the loss.

But grief is not something that becomes lighter through endurance alone.

Carrying grief silently does not make it smaller.
Sharing your grief appropriately often does.

Redefining Strength

Strength is often misunderstood.

Strength is not your ability to function without support.
Strength is not your absence of need.
Strength is not your silence.

Strength is recognizing when something matters enough to be tended with care.

Seeking help is not weakness.
It is **wisdom**.

It is an acknowledgment that your grief is real, that it has weight, and that no one is meant to carry it entirely alone.

What Support Can Look Like

Support does not look the same for everyone.

It may include:

- grief counseling or therapy
- support groups like the "Still With You" Grief Support Circle
- trusted friends or family
- spiritual or reflective guidance
- structured spaces for remembrance like an ancestor altar

Support does not erase grief.
It **changes how it is held**.

You do not need to decide everything at once. You do not need to know exactly what kind of help you need. Often, the first step is simply acknowledging that support could exist.

There Is No Deadline for Help

Many people wait until they feel "bad enough" to seek support.

There is no threshold you must cross.
There is no test you must pass.

You are allowed to seek help **before** you reach exhaustion.

Support is not a last resort.
It is a form of self-care.

Gentle Reflections (Optional)

You may engage with these reflections in any order, or not at all. They are offered as gentle invitations—not instructions.

Reflection 1: Naming the Weight

Pause for a moment.

Without trying to change anything, ask yourself:

- "How heavy does my grief feel right now?"

You might imagine a scale, a sensation, or simply a word.

There is no right answer. Awareness alone is meaningful.

Reflection 2: Listening to a Signal

Review the signs discussed in this chapter:

- disrupted sleep
- isolation
- persistent guilt
- loss of meaning

If one stands out, acknowledge it gently.

You might say:

"This is something that deserves care."

No action is required yet.

Reflection 3: Reimagining Strength

Complete this sentence privately, in writing or thought:

- "Being strong right now could look like…"

Notice what comes up. There is no correct response.

Reflection 4: Imagining Support Without Commitment

Imagine support existing in a way that feels safe and manageable.

Ask yourself:

- "If support were available, what would I hope it would give me?"
- "What would make it feel less overwhelming?"

You are not deciding anything—only allowing possibility.

Reflection 5: Offering Yourself Permission

Place a hand over your heart or take one slow breath.

You might quietly say:

"I am allowed to need help."

Let the statement rest without judgment.

Closing This Chapter

Grief becomes heavy not because you are weak, but because you are human.

When the weight grows too much for one person to carry, support is not an admission of failure—it is an act of respect for what has been lost.

In the next chapter, we will explore how shared space, community, and being witnessed can ease grief's weight and remind us that even in loss, we do not disappear from one another's lives.

For now, it is enough to know this:

You were never meant to carry everything alone.

And you do not have to start now.

CHAPTER 6:
The Power of Community

Grief changes how it feels to exist in the world.

What once felt familiar to you may now feel distant. Ordinary conversations can feel strangely hollow. You may find yourself nodding, responding, even smiling—while feeling as though you are watching life from the outside.

You might be surrounded by people and still feel profoundly alone.

This is not because others do not care.
It is because grief creates an experience that words struggle to hold.

And when grief is held alone for too long, it becomes heavier.

Why Grief Pulls Us Into Isolation

After loss, many people withdraw—not because they want to be alone, but because they don't know how to be *with others* anymore.

They pull back because:

- they don't want to burden anyone
- they fear breaking down in front of others
- they are tired of hearing well-intentioned but painful phrases
- they don't know how to explain what has changed

Isolation often begins as protection.

It is the nervous system's way of saying, *This is too much right now.*

But grief was never meant to be carried entirely in silence.

A Story of Silent Grief

There was a woman who joined a grief support space and said nothing for weeks.

She logged in. She listened. She left quietly.

One day, after hearing others share stories that echoed her own, she finally spoke. Her voice shook as she said, "I didn't think anyone would understand how lonely this feels, even when people are around."

What followed was not advice.
No one tried to fix her pain.
No one rushed her words.

There was simply recognition.

Later, she shared that hearing others speak had slowly loosened something inside her. She hadn't realized how much energy she had been using to hold everything together on her own.

Being witnessed did not remove her grief—but it made it **bearable**.

The Human Need to Be Witnessed

One of the most powerful aspects of community is not conversation or guidance.

It is **being witnessed**.

To be witnessed means:

- someone listens without correcting you
- your pain is not minimized or compared
- your emotions are allowed to exist as they are
- silence is honored

When grief is witnessed, the nervous system receives a quiet message:

I am not alone with this.

That message can soften pain in ways nothing else can.

When Well-Meaning Words of Support Hurt

Many grieving people avoid community because they have already been hurt by it.

They have heard:

- "Everything happens for a reason."
- "They wouldn't want you to be sad."
- "It was just their time."
- "You have to stay strong."

Even when spoken with love, these words can feel like pressure—to heal faster, to feel differently, to be someone other than who you are.

When this happens, withdrawal can feel safer.

But healthy community does not rush grief.
It does not reframe pain prematurely.
It does not demand hope.

Healthy community **makes room**.

Another Story: Grief That Needed Witnessing

There was a man who lost his partner suddenly. Friends tried to help, but their discomfort showed. Conversations stayed surface-level. Invitations stopped coming after a few months.

He began to believe that his grief had an expiration date.

In a shared grief space, he finally said aloud, "I still talk to them in my head. I don't know if that's okay."

No one laughed.
No one corrected him.
Someone simply said, "That makes sense."

That sentence stayed with him.

Not because it explained anything—but because it **allowed** something.

Grief does not need permission to exist. But we often need permission to stop hiding it.

What Community Does—and Does Not—Require

True support does not require:

- telling your story before you're ready
- believing the same things as others

- speaking when silence feels safer
- presenting your grief in a certain way

In healthy community:

- listening is participation
- presence is enough
- stepping back is respected
- returning later is welcomed

Some people speak often.
Some speak once.
Some never speak at all.

All are welcome.

Community as a Container, Not a Cure

Community does not erase grief.

It does not undo loss.
It does not provide answers to unanswerable questions.
It does not replace what was taken.

What it does is **contain grief**.

Containment means:

- emotions have somewhere to land
- pain does not circulate endlessly inside you
- love can be shared instead of sealed away

Grief becomes heavier when it has nowhere to go.

Community gives it a place to rest.

Still With You Grief Support Circle: A Calm Place to Land

This understanding is why Still With You Grief Support Circle offers a **free, moderated grief support community**.

The intention is simple:

- to reduce isolation
- to create steadiness
- to offer a place where grief does not need to be explained

There is:

- no pressure to share
- no belief requirements
- no expectation to perform healing
- no timeline

You may come to speak.
You may come to listen.
You may come simply to sit among others who understand.

All of these are enough.

Why Moderation Matters

Grief spaces must be protected.

Moderation ensures:

- emotional safety
- respect for different experiences
- no one is rushed or corrected
- grief is not turned into debate

This allows people to show up honestly—without bracing themselves.

Love Is Not Meant to Be Carried Alone

Grief can quietly convince us that love must now be carried privately, carefully, and alone.

Community gently reminds us otherwise.

When love is shared—through stories, silence, or simple presence—it becomes lighter. Not because it matters less, but because it is held by more than one heart.

Grief does not shrink when hidden.
It softens when witnessed.

Gentle Reflections & Self-Love Exercises (Optional)

You may choose one, many, or none of these. They are invitations only.

Reflection 1: Checking Your Capacity for Connection

Ask yourself gently:

- "How much connection feels possible for me right now?"

Your answer may be:

- very little
- some
- changing day by day

There is no wrong capacity.

Reflection 2: Noticing Isolation Without Judgment

Consider:

- "When I am alone, does my grief feel steadier—or heavier?"

There is no correct preference. This reflection is simply information.

Reflection 3: A Self-Love Statement

Place a hand over your heart or take one slow breath.

Silently say:

"I am allowed to need others, and I am allowed to take my time."

Let the words rest without trying to feel anything.

Reflection 4: Imagining Being Witnessed

Without committing to action, imagine a space where your grief would be welcomed exactly as it is.

Ask yourself:

- What would *not* be expected of me there?
- What would help me feel safe?

You are not deciding anything—only noticing.

Reflection 5: A Small Act of Kindness Toward Yourself

Choose one small act of care today:

- resting
- stepping outside
- drinking water
- allowing yourself to stop

Self-love does not need to be dramatic. It only needs to be sincere.

Closing This Chapter

Grief is not meant to be carried alone.

Community does not demand readiness, belief, or strength. It offers presence.

And sometimes, presence is enough to remind us that even in loss, we still belong.

In the next chapter, we will explore how legacy and remembrance can help love move forward without leaving grief behind.

For now, remember this:

You are not alone in what you are carrying.
And you do not have to be.

You Don't Have to Walk This Alone

If you are longing for connection,
reflection, and steady companionship in your grief journey,
you are invited to join the **Still With You Grief Support Circle.**

A quiet space for conversation, remembrance, and healing — at your own pace.

Visit the
Still With You Grief Support
Circle on Facebook

Visit the
Still With You Grief Support
Circle on TikTok

CHAPTER 7: Honoring Love Forward

When someone we love dies, grief often feels like the end of something.

The end of a voice.
The end of shared routines.
The end of a future imagined together.

But over time—sometimes very slowly, sometimes unexpectedly—another truth begins to emerge:

Love does not end.
It changes direction.

Honoring love forward is not about leaving grief behind. It is about allowing love to continue having influence, shape, and presence in your life—even as everything has changed.

Legacy Is Not Only What Is Left Behind

When people hear the word *legacy*, they often think of large gestures or formal inheritances—things written down or passed on materially.

But a person's legacy is much quieter than that.

Legacy lives in:

- how someone taught you to treat others
- the values that they modeled without words
- the way that they made you feel safe, seen, or challenged

- the habits that you still carry because of them

Legacy is not something that you receive all at once. It is something that you **live into**, often without realizing it.

Every time that you act with kindness that was learned from them, you are honoring their legacy.

A Story of Legacy in Small Things

There was a woman who lost her grandmother, the person who had raised her.

For a long time, she felt frozen—unsure how to move forward without the person who had anchored her sense of home. One day, while cleaning her kitchen, she realized she was folding towels the same way her grandmother always had.

It stopped her.

She hadn't chosen to do it that way. She had simply absorbed it.

In that moment, she realized something important: her grandmother was not only in her memories. She was in her gestures, her rhythms, her care for ordinary things.

That realization did not remove the grief—but it softened it.

Legacy, she realized, was already alive.

Memory as a Living Presence

Memory is often misunderstood as something fixed—snapshots of the past stored away.

In grief, memory is far more active.

Memories surface unexpectedly. They change over time. They become less sharp in some places and more meaningful in others. This is not forgetting—it is **integration**.

Memory allows love to remain dynamic rather than frozen in pain.

You are allowed to remember:

- joy without guilt
- laughter without apology
- warmth without fear that it diminishes loss

Memory does not betray grief.
It gives grief room to breathe.

Passing Values Forward

One of the most powerful ways love moves forward is through values.

Values are not possessions.
They are ways of being.

You may find yourself:

- showing patience you learned from them
- standing up for something they cared about
- offering comfort the way they once offered it to you

Passing values forward does not require conscious effort. It happens naturally when love has shaped you deeply.

In this way, love becomes **directional**—moving outward, influencing others, shaping futures that your loved one will never physically see, but will still touch.

Another Story: Love That Continued Its Work

There was a father who lost his son suddenly.

For months, he felt hollow. Nothing felt meaningful. Then one afternoon, he overheard a neighbor struggling with a situation his son had once helped him through years earlier.

Without thinking, the father stepped in—offering guidance, reassurance, and steady presence.

Later that evening, he realized something quietly profound.

He had just spoken with his son's voice—not literally, but through the values his son had lived by.

That moment did not erase the loss. But it reminded him that love does not stop working simply because our loved one is physically gone.

When Love Encounters What Was Left Unfinished

Many people carry a quiet weight after experiencing loss—not only grief, but the feeling that something was left undone.

Unfinished affairs can take many forms:

- conversations never had
- apologies never spoken
- wishes never expressed
- practical matters left unresolved

These unfinished elements often surface later, not as crises, but as lingering discomfort or unease.

Honoring love forward does not require solving everything at once. Sometimes it begins simply by acknowledging that something remains incomplete—and that it matters.

Acknowledgment is not obligation.
It is awareness.

Honoring Love Without Pressure

There is no solitary correct way for you to honor love forward.

Some people do it actively—through service, advocacy, or creative expression. Others do it quietly—through private remembrance, changed priorities, or gentler ways of living.

You are not required to:

- make meaning immediately
- transform your pain into purpose
- "do something" with your grief

Love moves forward at its own pace.

Sometimes honoring love simply means continuing to live—imperfectly, honestly, and with care.

Love as a Companion, Not a Weight

Grief often convinces us that carrying love forward will be heavy.

But love does not need to be carried like a burden.

Over time, love can transform to become:

- a quiet guide
- a steady influence
- a source of resilience

It can walk beside you rather than sit on your chest.

This does not happen all at once. It happens gradually, as grief loosens its grip and love finds new ways to exist.

Gentle Reflections & Self-Love Exercises (Optional)

These exercises are invitations only. You may choose one, several, or none. There is no expectation to complete them.

Reflection 1: Noticing Legacy Already Present

Take a quiet moment and ask yourself:

- "In what small ways has this person already shaped how I live?"

You might notice:

- habits
- values
- reactions
- ways of caring

There is no need to write anything down unless it feels helpful.

Reflection 2: Memory Without Judgment

Bring to mind one memory—pleasant or painful.

Notice:

- how it feels in your body
- whether it brings warmth, sadness, or both

You are not required to analyze it.

Allow the memory to exist without deciding what it means.

Reflection 3: Values You Carry Forward

Complete this sentence privately:

- "Something they taught me—directly or indirectly—was…"

Notice how that value shows up in your life today.

Reflection 4: Acknowledging the Unfinished (Gently)

If something feels unfinished, you might ask:

- "What feels unresolved—not to fix it, but to name it?"

You do not need to take action. Naming it is enough for now. Naming it helps you to know what you are sitting with.

Reflection 5: A Self-Love Pause

Place one hand over your heart or take one slow breath.

Silently say:

"I am allowed to honor love in ways that feel right for me."

Let the words settle without expectation.

Reflection 6: Looking Forward Without Forcing Meaning

Imagine the coming months—not with plans or goals, but with curiosity.

Ask yourself:

- "What would it feel like to let love walk with me, rather than weigh me down?"

There is no answer required.

Closing This Chapter

Honoring love forward does not mean leaving grief behind.

It means allowing love to continue shaping your life—even in its absence.

Legacy lives in you.
Memory breathes through you.
Values move forward because you carry them.

And even when something feels unfinished, love remains capable of guiding what comes next.

In the final chapter, we will reflect on integration—how grief and love can coexist without canceling each other out.

For now, remember this:

Love did not end.
It changed direction.
And you are allowed to let it move forward—gently.

PART II:

CARRYING GRIEF FORWARD

Gentle Daily Grief Check-Ins

DAY 1 — Arriving Where You Are

Today is not about understanding grief.
It is about arriving honestly where you are.

Grief often comes with an internal pressure to orient yourself quickly—to figure out what this loss means, how it will change you, and how you are supposed to live with it. That pressure can feel exhausting before the day has even begun.

So today, you are not asked to orient yourself.

You are only asked to arrive.

Arrival means acknowledging what is true right now, without judgment or urgency. It means noticing how your body feels as you begin the day. It means recognizing whether grief feels loud, quiet, confusing, or distant.

There is no right way for grief to show up on Day One—or Day One thousand.

If emotions feel strong today, that does not mean you are overwhelmed.
If emotions feel muted today, that does not mean you are avoiding anything.

Grief adapts moment by moment.

Today may feel unreal. It may feel heavy. It may feel strangely ordinary. Any of these experiences are allowed.

You do not need to carry yesterday's grief forward, and you do not need to prepare for tomorrow's. You are only here.

If your mind begins to race—asking how long this will last or who you will become—gently return to now. Grief becomes more manageable when it is held in smaller pieces.

Today, the smallest piece is enough.

Optional Reflection

- "Right now, I feel…"
- "What feels most present in my body today is…"
- "What I am allowed to release today is…"

Close by reminding yourself:

I am allowed to arrive exactly as I am.

DAY 2 — Letting the Day Be What It Is

Grief often brings a quiet resistance to the day itself.

You may wake up and feel disappointed that the world has continued. You may feel pressure to engage with responsibilities that now feel meaningless or overwhelming. You may wish the day would simply pass without requiring anything from you.

Today does not need to be shaped.

You are allowed to let this day be what it is.

Some days grief demands attention. Other days it sits quietly in the background. Neither experience is more "correct" than the other.

If you feel functional today, that does not mean you are forgetting.
If you feel undone today, that does not mean you are failing.

Grief does not follow a pattern that can be predicted or managed.

Today might include moments of distraction, moments of sadness, or moments of nothing at all. Each moment belongs.

If guilt appears—about what you should be doing or feeling—notice it gently and set it aside. Guilt often appears when love has nowhere to go.

You do not need to make today meaningful. You only need to let it unfold.

If rest feels possible, rest.
If movement feels supportive, move.
If stillness feels safer, choose stillness.

The day does not need your interpretation. It only needs your presence.

Optional Reflection

- "Today feels like…"
- "One thing I can allow myself today is…"
- "One expectation I can loosen today is…"

Close with:

I do not need to shape this day for it to be valid.

DAY 3 — Listening Without Fixing

Grief often comes with an urge to solve itself.

You may notice thoughts that sound like:

- "I should be handling this better."
- "I should be further along."
- "I should feel different by now."

These thoughts often come from a place of wanting relief, not from truth.

Today is an invitation to listen without fixing.

Listening means noticing what arises—emotion, thought, sensation—without trying to change it or explain it. It means allowing grief to speak in its own language.

You are not required to respond to grief with insight. You are not required to transform pain into meaning.

Sometimes grief simply needs space.

If sadness appears today, allow it to exist without asking it to leave. If anger appears, let it stand without judgment. If numbness appears, trust that it is serving a purpose.

Listening without fixing does not mean you are passive. It means you are offering yourself the same patience you would offer someone you love.

Grief softens when it is not argued with.

Today, see if you can notice one moment—however brief—where you allow an emotion to exist without commentary.

That moment counts.

Optional Reflection

- "Something I notice without judging today is…"
- "An emotion I can allow today is…"
- "What listening feels like in my body is…"

Close with:

I am allowed to listen without fixing.

DAY 4 — Making Space for Rest

Grief is exhausting.

Even when nothing is happening, grief consumes energy. It asks the nervous system to process loss, uncertainty, and change all at once. Fatigue is not a sign of weakness—it is a sign of effort.

Today is about making space for rest.

Rest does not always mean sleep. It can mean pausing, simplifying, or choosing not to engage. It can mean allowing yourself to stop before you feel depleted.

If rest feels difficult or undeserved, notice that resistance with kindness. Many people were taught that rest must be earned. Grief challenges that belief.

Rest is not something you earn in grief. It is something you need.

If possible, choose one small way to rest today:

- sitting without distraction
- lying down for a few minutes
- stepping outside

- allowing yourself to stop one task early

You do not need to justify this rest.

Grief requires more care, not less.

Optional Reflection

- “Rest for me today could look like…”
- “One thing I can stop doing today is…”
- “My body is asking for…”

Close with:

Rest is a form of care, not a reward.

DAY 5 — Noticing What Still Supports You

Grief can make the world feel stripped of its supports.

Things that once brought comfort may feel distant or ineffective. This can be frightening, as though nothing remains steady.

Today is an invitation to notice—even quietly—what still supports you.

Support does not have to be profound. It can be small and ordinary:

- a familiar routine
- a warm drink
- a window of light
- a voice you trust

These supports may not remove grief, but they help you remain oriented within it.

Notice if there is one thing today that feels even slightly stabilizing. You do not need to hold onto it or recreate it perfectly. Simply noticing matters.

Grief does not require that everything feel supportive. It only asks that something does.

Optional Reflection

- "One thing that feels steady today is…"
- "Support shows up for me today as…"
- "Something that helps me feel grounded is…"

Close with:

Even now, something supports me.

DAY 6 — Allowing Mixed Emotions

Grief rarely arrives alone.

It often brings contradictory feelings—sadness and relief, longing and peace, anger and gratitude. These combinations can feel confusing or even unsettling.

Today is about allowing mixed emotions to exist together.

You are not required to choose one feeling over another. Emotions do not cancel each other out.

Feeling moments of ease does not diminish loss. Feeling moments of pain does not erase healing.

Mixed emotions are a sign that your inner world is complex and alive.

If you notice yourself judging an emotion today, pause and soften that judgment. Emotions do not need to be consistent to be valid.

Optional Reflection

- "Two emotions I notice today are…"
- "Allowing mixed feelings feels like…"
- "I can let these emotions coexist without deciding anything."

Close with:

I am allowed to feel more than one thing at once.

DAY 7 — Ending the Week Gently

Reaching the end of this first week does not mean you have completed anything.

There is no milestone to reach in grief. There is no finish line.

Today is simply a pause.

Notice what this week has been like—not to evaluate it, but to acknowledge that you have lived through it.

You may feel tired.
You may feel unchanged.
You may feel subtly different.

All of these experiences are valid.

Grief unfolds slowly. It responds to patience more than effort.

As you close this week, see if you can offer yourself a moment of recognition—not for progress, but for presence.

You are still here.

Optional Reflection

- "This week has felt…"
- "One thing I can acknowledge myself for is…"
- "As I move into the next days, I allow…"

Close with:

I am allowed to move forward gently.

DAY 8 — Making Room for Memory

As grief settles into its longer rhythm, memories often begin to surface more frequently.

Sometimes they arrive gently. Other times they appear without warning and bring a wave of emotion with them. This can feel unsettling, especially if you worry that remembering will make the pain stronger.

Today is about making room for memory—without forcing it and without resisting it.

Memory is not an enemy of healing.
It is one of the ways love continues to exist.

You are not required to seek memories today. But if one appears, you are allowed to let it stay for a moment. You do not need to analyze it or decide what it means.

If a memory brings sadness, allow the sadness.
If a memory brings warmth, allow the warmth.
If a memory brings both, that is also allowed.

Grief often teaches us to fear memory, as though remembering will pull us backward. In truth, memory often helps grief move *through* us rather than remain stuck.

If a memory feels overwhelming, you are allowed to step away. You are not obligated to stay with it longer than feels safe.

Memory does not need to be honored perfectly. It only needs permission.

Today, notice whether a memory arises on its own. If it does, consider letting it exist briefly, without judgment.

Optional Reflection

- "A memory that came to mind today was…"
- "This memory made me feel…"
- "What I notice in my body when I remember is…"

Close with:

I am allowed to remember at my own pace.

DAY 9 — When Grief Feels Quiet

Not every day of grief feels dramatic or intense.

Some days feel strangely quiet.

Quiet days can bring confusion. You may wonder whether something is wrong, whether you are avoiding grief, or whether the pain is waiting to return unexpectedly.

Today is about honoring quiet without suspicion.

Quiet does not mean absence.
Quiet does not mean forgetting.
Quiet often means your nervous system is resting.

Grief is not meant to be experienced at full intensity all the time. Your body needs pauses in order to integrate what has been felt.

If today feels calm or neutral, allow that calm. You do not need to brace yourself for what comes next.

Quiet is not betrayal.
It is part of how grief breathes.

If guilt arises about feeling okay today, notice it gently and let it pass. Love does not require constant suffering to remain real.

Today, see if you can allow quiet to exist without questioning it.

Optional Reflection

- "Today feels quieter than usual because…"
- "What quiet allows me to do is…"
- "Something I can appreciate about this quiet is…"

Close with:

Quiet is allowed. I do not need to explain it.

DAY 10 — The Body Carries Grief Too

Grief does not live only in thoughts or emotions. It lives in the body.

You may notice:

- fatigue
- tension
- aches
- restlessness
- heaviness

These sensations are not signs that something is wrong. They are signs that your body is processing loss.

Today is about listening to your body without judgment.

Rather than asking, "What's wrong with me?"
You might gently ask, "What is my body responding to?"

Grief asks the nervous system to adapt to a world that has changed. That adaptation takes energy.

If your body feels tired today, that is information.
If it feels restless, that is information.
If it feels numb, that is information too.

You are not required to fix your body. You are only invited to notice it with kindness.

If possible, offer your body one small act of care today:

- stretching
- warmth

- hydration
- stillness

Care does not need to be elaborate in order to be effective.

Optional Reflection

- "Something my body is asking for today is…"
- "Where I feel grief physically is…"
- "One way I can respond gently to my body is…"

Close with:

My body is part of my grief, and it deserves care.

DAY 11 — When Others Seem to Move On

One of the quieter pains of grief is noticing that others appear to move on more quickly.

You may feel surprised by how soon the world resumes its normal pace. Conversations shift. Schedules fill. People stop asking how you are.

This can feel isolating.

Today is about acknowledging that your timeline does not need to match anyone else's.

Grief does not follow social expectations. It follows attachment.

If you notice resentment or loneliness today, allow those feelings without judgment. They are often responses to feeling left behind rather than signs of bitterness.

You are allowed to still be grieving—even if others are not.

You do not owe anyone an explanation for the pace of your healing.

Optional Reflection

- "Something that feels difficult when others move on is…"
- "What I wish others understood about my grief is…"
- "What helps me feel less alone in this moment is…"

Close with:

My grief has its own timing, and that is allowed.

DAY 12 — Letting Joy Visit Briefly

Joy can feel complicated after loss.

Moments of laughter, ease, or pleasure may arrive unexpectedly—and be followed by guilt or sadness.

Today is about allowing joy to visit briefly, without interrogation.

Joy does not replace grief.
It does not erase love.
It does not signal forgetting.

Joy is not something you must invite or reject. It comes when it comes.

If joy appears today, see if you can let it stay for a moment—without asking it to justify itself.

Grief and joy can coexist. One does not cancel the other.

Optional Reflection

- "A moment of ease I noticed today was…"
- "How my body responds to joy right now is…"
- "What allows me to receive joy without guilt is…"

Close with:

Joy is allowed to visit, even here.

DAY 13 — Naming What Still Hurts

Some aspects of grief remain tender long after others soften.

Certain memories, dates, or thoughts may still bring sharp pain.

Today is about naming what still hurts—without trying to fix it.

Naming is not the same as dwelling.
Naming is a form of honesty.

If there is something you have been avoiding acknowledging, consider gently naming it today. You do not need to act on it. You do not need to share it.

Recognition alone can reduce the burden of carrying it silently.

Optional Reflection

- "Something that still hurts is…"
- "When I name this, I feel…"
- "What helps me carry this pain is…"

Close with:

I am allowed to name what hurts without solving it.

DAY 14 — Reaching the Middle Gently

You have reached the midpoint of these daily check-ins.

This does not mean you are halfway through grief. It simply means you have been showing up with honesty and care.

Today is a moment to pause.

Notice what has changed, if anything—not to measure progress, but to acknowledge presence.

You may feel steadier.
You may feel the same.
You may feel different in ways that you cannot yet name.

All are valid.

Grief unfolds over time, shaped by patience more than effort.

Today, see if you can offer yourself recognition—not for improvement, but for endurance.

You are still here.

Optional Reflection

- "Something I notice now that I didn't before is…"
- "What I can acknowledge myself for is…"
- "As I continue, I allow myself to…"

Close with:

I am allowed to continue at my own pace.

DAY 15 — Learning How to Carry This

By now, you may be noticing that grief is no longer something you wake up *into* each day—it is something you wake up *with*.

This shift can be subtle. It does not mean the grief is smaller or easier. It means you are beginning to carry it differently.

Carrying grief does not mean accepting what happened.
It does not mean approving of the loss.
It means acknowledging that this experience is now part of your life's landscape.

Today is about noticing *how* you are carrying grief.

Is it pressed tightly against you?
Is it held at a distance?
Does it feel heavier in some moments than others?

There is no correct way to carry grief. There is only the way that allows you to continue breathing, living, and responding to the world around you.

If you notice moments where grief feels slightly less consuming, you do not need to explain them. They are not a sign that grief is fading—they are a sign that your capacity is expanding.

Capacity does not mean strength.
It means accommodation.

Grief becomes more bearable not because it disappears, but because you slowly grow around it.

Optional Reflection

- "Today, grief feels like it is sitting…"
- "What makes carrying grief slightly easier is…"
- "Something that I am learning about myself through this is…"

Close with:

I am learning how to carry this in my own way.

DAY 16 — Allowing Yourself to Be Changed

Loss changes people.

Not all at once.
Not in obvious ways.
But steadily, quietly, and deeply.

Today is about allowing yourself to acknowledge that you have been changed—without deciding whether that change is good or bad.

You may notice:

- different priorities
- less tolerance for trivial things
- deeper empathy
- unexpected fragility
- unexpected strength

Change does not mean you are no longer yourself. It means you are responding honestly to what you have lived through.

You are not required to "return" to who you were before. That person lived in a different world.

Grief asks you to become someone new—not better, not worse, just *more informed by love and loss*.

If this realization brings sadness, allow it.
If it brings clarity, allow that too.

You are not betraying the past by changing.
You are responding to it.

Optional Reflection

- "One way I notice myself changing is…"
- "What feels unfamiliar about me now is…"
- "What I want to honor about who I am becoming is…"

Close with:

I am allowed to be changed by love and loss.

DAY 17 — When Grief and Life Coexist

There may be moments now when grief and ordinary life exist side by side.

You may run errands while carrying sadness.
You may laugh and then feel a wave of longing or tears.
You may feel almost normal—and then not.

Today is about allowing coexistence.

Grief does not need to dominate every moment to remain real. Life does not need to stop in order to respect loss.

Coexistence is not forgetting.
It is adaptation.

You are allowed to:

- care about new things
- feel engaged at times
- step back into life unevenly

Grief does not demand exclusivity. It asks for honesty.

If coexistence feels uncomfortable or confusing, that is natural. It takes time to trust that life can continue without diminishing what was lost.

Today, notice one moment where grief and life intersect—without judgment.

Optional Reflection

- “Today, grief and life showed up together when…”
- “What feels hardest about coexistence is…”
- “What feels relieving about coexistence is…”

Close with:

I am allowed to live while I grieve.

DAY 18 — Honoring Love Forward

Grief often keeps love facing backward—toward what was.

Today is about noticing how love may also be moving forward.

Honoring love forward does not require action or purpose. It often happens quietly.

You may notice yourself:

- speaking with greater kindness
- choosing what matters more carefully
- responding with empathy you learned through loss

These are not compensations.
They are continuations.

Love does not end with death. It changes direction.

If today you notice a moment where love influences how you move through the world, allow yourself to acknowledge it—without pressure to do more.

Honoring love forward is not a task.
It is a way love continues to live.

Optional Reflection

- "One way love shows up in me now is…"
- "Something I do differently because of this love is…"
- "What honoring love forward feels like today is…"

Close with:

Love still has a direction, and I am part of it.

DAY 19 — Making Peace With Unanswered Questions

Some questions will never have answers.

Grief often leaves behind:

- "Why?"
- "What if?"
- "If only..."

These questions can circle endlessly, searching for something solid to land on.

Today is about allowing questions to exist without demanding resolution.

Unanswered questions do not mean you failed to understand. They mean the situation exceeds explanation.

Peace does not come from answering every question. It often comes from loosening the grip on needing answers in order to move forward.

If questions arise today, notice them gently. You do not need to argue with them or follow them.

Some questions can be carried without being solved.

Optional Reflection

- "A question I still carry is..."
- "How it feels to let this question remain unanswered is..."
- "What helps me live alongside uncertainty is..."

Close with:

I am allowed to live without every answer.

DAY 20 — Trusting Your Pace

By now, you may be feeling pressure—from yourself or others—to know where you are headed.

Today is about trusting your pace.

Grief does not move in predictable stages. It unfolds in response to readiness, not expectation.

You are not late.
You are not behind.
You are not doing this wrong.

Your pace is shaped by love, attachment, and the depth of what was lost.

Trust does not mean certainty. It means allowing yourself to move forward without forcing direction.

Today, notice if you are judging your pace. If so, soften that judgment.

You are allowed to take the time you need.

Optional Reflection

- "Something about my pace I can accept is…"
- "What I don't need to rush right now is…"
- "Trusting myself today looks like…"

Close with:

My pace is allowed to be exactly what it is.

DAY 21 — Carrying Grief Forward With You

Today marks the end of these daily check-ins—but not the end of grief.

Grief does not end. It integrates.

Integration means grief becomes part of your story rather than the whole story. It means you learn how to carry love and loss alongside living.

As you reach this day, you are not expected to feel different. You are only invited to acknowledge that you have shown up—day after day—with honesty and care.

That matters.

Grief does not ask for perfection. It asks for presence.

Today, take a moment to recognize yourself—not for healing, not for progress, but for endurance.

You are still here.
You are still carrying love.
You are still becoming.

Optional Reflection

- "What I carry forward from these days is…"
- "What I want to continue offering myself is…"
- "As I move forward, I allow…"

Close with:

I can carry this and still live.

Letters You May Never Send

Words That Still Need Somewhere to Go

There are often things left unsaid after loss.

Not because you didn't care.
Not because you didn't try.
But because life does not always give us the timing we expect.

Grief carries unfinished conversations.
Words that had no place to land.
Feelings that never found a moment.

These letters are not meant to be mailed.
They are not meant to be perfect.
They are not meant to resolve anything.

They exist to give what remains **a place to rest**.

You may write these letters.
You may read them silently.
You may listen and never pick up a pen.

All are valid.

There is no requirement to complete every letter.
There is no requirement to feel better afterward.

These letters are invitations—nothing more.

Letter One:

To the One I Lost

You may begin this letter in any way that feels natural.

You might write:

- their name
- "Dear you"
- or nothing at all

This letter is a space to say what never had the chance to be spoken.

You might include:

- things you wish you had said
- moments you still replay
- gratitude
- anger
- love that still feels unfinished

There is no need to be kind or composed.
Honesty matters more than tone.

You may find that emotions shift as you write. That is normal. You can stop at any point.

If it feels right, you may close the letter with:

- "I miss you."
- "I'm still here."
- or no closing at all

This letter does not need to be reread.
It does not need to be kept.

Its purpose is expression—not preservation.

Letter Two:

To What I Never Got to Say

Some grief is not about the person alone, but about **the moments that never happened**.

This letter is for:

- conversations that were postponed
- apologies that never found their moment
- questions that went unanswered
- hopes that never unfolded

You might write to:

- the moment that never came
- the future you imagined
- the version of life that changed suddenly

This letter can hold disappointment, longing, or sorrow without explanation.

You are not required to forgive anything here.
You are not required to make peace.

Naming what didn't happen is a form of acknowledgment.

Acknowledgment is not bitterness.
It is honesty.

Letter Three:

To Myself Before the Loss

Grief often carries a quiet tenderness for who we once were.

This letter is written to the version of you who lived **before** this loss entered your life.

You might write about:

- what that version of you did not yet know
- what you wish you could have prepared them for
- compassion you now feel for their innocence

You may notice grief soften here, replaced by gentleness.

You might offer reassurance.
You might offer understanding.
You might simply witness who you were.

This letter often reveals how deeply loss changes us—and how much care we deserve for having lived through it.

Letter Four

To Myself Now

This letter is for the person you are becoming in grief.

You may write about:

- how hard this has been
- what feels most exhausting
- what you wish others understood
- what you are proud of surviving

You may speak with kindness or frustration. Both belong here.

If words are difficult, you may write only a few lines.

Sometimes the most important thing we can do is **acknowledge ourselves**.

This letter is not about encouragement or optimism.
It is about recognition.

Letter Five:

To the Guilt I Carry

Guilt often lingers quietly in grief.

This letter is for guilt—not as an enemy, but as something to be understood.

You may write about:

- what you feel guilty for
- what you wish had been different
- what you feel responsible for

Then, if it feels possible, you might gently ask:

- "What are you protecting me from?"
- "What would you say if you could speak fully?"

You do not need to resolve guilt here.
You are simply listening.

Sometimes guilt softens when it is allowed to speak.

Letter Six:

To the Love That Remains

This letter is not about loss—it is about continuity.

You may write about:

- how love still shows up
- how it has changed
- how it surprises you

You may write about how love feels heavier, quieter, or different.

This letter is a reminder that love does not disappear when someone dies. It adapts.

Writing this letter does not diminish grief.
It acknowledges what grief exists because of.

Letter Seven (Optional)

A Letter You Don't Yet Have Words For

If none of the letters above feel right, this space is for what has not yet taken shape.

You may write fragments.
You may write questions.
You may write nothing at all.

Even sitting with the page is a form of listening.

Gentle Guidance for This Section

- You do not need to complete these letters in order.
- You do not need to finish any letter in one sitting.
- You do not need to share these letters with anyone.

You may:

- keep them
- destroy them
- return to them later
- never return at all

All choices are valid.

Closing This Section

There are things grief cannot say out loud.

Letters give those things somewhere to go.

They do not close grief.
They do not complete it.

They make space.

If you choose to write, write gently.
If you choose not to, that is also a form of care.

In the next section, the book will move into quieter language—poems meant to sit beside you without asking anything in return.

For now, remember this:

You are allowed to speak what remains.
And you are allowed to rest afterward.

PART III:

FOR THE QUIET MOMENTS

1. The World Did Not Stop

The world did not stop
the day you were gone.
Morning still came,
and the night still moved on.

Cars filled the streets,
and strangers still smiled,
while I stood unmoving,
a stunned, grieving child.

It felt so unfair—
like a rule had been bent.
How could life go on
when my heart was spent?

I learned grief is standing
while time keeps its pace,
learning to breathe
in an altered place.

Some days I fall.
Some days I cope.
Some days just standing
is courage and hope.

2. I Still Say Your Name

I still say your name
when the room is still,
not to call you back,
but because I will.

Your name is a tether,
not a chain or a plea.
It anchors the love
that still lives in me.

I speak it in silence,
in whispers, in prayer—
not because you're lost,
but because you were there.

Your name does not trap me
in sorrow or pain.
It reminds me of love—
and I say it again.

3. The Weight I Carry

Grief has no shape,
yet it knows where to land,
a weight on my chest
That I never planned.

Some days it cuts sharp,
some days it just stays,
some days it waits
for the end of my days.

I'm learning I don't
have to hold it all tight,
I can set it down briefly—
for a breath, for a night.

The weight still exists,
but so do I too.
And I'm learning to live
while still missing you.

4. What Remains

What remains is not only
a picture or name,
not a moment replayed
or a flickering flame.

What remains is the kindness
I didn’t yet see,
the patience I carry
because you taught me.

You didn’t leave emptiness,
you left me aware
of what truly matters,
of how deeply I care.

What remains is not loss—
though loss still remains—
but love, learning
new shapes through the pain.

5. The Day I Laughed Again

The day that I laughed
caught me off my guard,
like joy had arrived
when the road was still hard.

I waited for guilt
to tell me I'd strayed,
that laughter meant love
was somehow betrayed.

But laughter did not
erase what was true,
it didn't replace
the love I had for you.

It was life reminding me,
gentle, not loud,
that loving you deeply
doesn't mean sorrow is vowed.

6. There Is No Pace

They tell me healing
moves straight like a line—
those words never came
from a love such as mine.

My grief circles back,
then rests, then returns,
it softens, it sharpens,
it aches, and it yearns.

There's no finish, no marker,
no time I must race—
there's only the rhythm
of my heart's own pace.

I'm learning to trust it,
slow, tender, and true—
there's no right way to miss
somebody like you.

7. I Carry You Forward

I once carried you
in plans and in days,
in routines, in futures,
in "one day" and "always."

Now I carry you quieter,
in choices I make,
in kindness I offer,
in pauses I take.

I'm not holding on—
I'm not stuck in before.
I'm holding you forward,
still loving you more.

The way that I carry you
has changed its design,
but love does not fade—
it just learns to align.

8. When the Night Is Long

When the night stretches long
and the house speaks your name,
before I'm prepared
for the ache to return again,

I remind myself softly,
no answers are due,
no meaning is needed
to get myself through.

I only need permission
to feel what I feel,
to let sorrow be honest,
to let breathing be real.

Morning will come,
but until that time,
I'm allowed to be here—
still loving, still mine.

9. The Shape of Tomorrow

I do not know yet
what tomorrow will bring,
what shape it will take,
or what songs it will sing.

I only know this—
though the road feels unclear,
I am still standing
and still drawing near

to moments of peace
that arrive without sound,
to days where my feet
feel steadier on the ground.

Hope doesn't shout.
It doesn't demand.
It waits like a light
I can hold in my hand.

10. Still Becoming

I am not who I was
before grief came through,
but I am not finished—
I'm still becoming new.

Some pieces feel fragile,
some feel more strong,
some feel like they've waited
their whole life this long

to rise from the quiet,
to step into view,
shaped by the love
that I once shared with you.

I am becoming—not better,
not fixed, not complete—
just more awake
to what makes life sweet.

11. Love Did Not Leave

Love did not leave
when your voice went quiet.
It changed how it speaks—
less urgent, more private.

It speaks in my choices,
in how I forgive,
in the gentler ways
I'm learning to live.

Love did not vanish,
did not dissolve—
it didn't need answers
to continue to evolve.

It stayed.
It grew roots.
It learned how to be
a steady companion
still walking with me.

12. I Will Be Okay (In My Own Way)

I won't promise myself
that I won't cry today

I won't try to pretend

I know what to say.

But I promise this—
as I am walking this way

I will be honest about my emotions

No matter what way they sway

I will be alright
not because I forgot,
but because I remembered
how deeply I thought,

how fiercely I loved,
how honestly I stay—
and that kind of love
will still carry my way.

Conclusion

You Are Still Here

If you have reached this place at last,
you have stayed through shadow, ache, and past.
Not because the pain grew small or thin,
but because you stayed—and stayed within.

You stayed when days felt hard to bear,
when love hurt more than empty air,
when memory came without a cue
and took you back to life with you.

You stayed.

Grief did not ask before it came,
it never knocks, it never waits.
But here it learned—through loss and care—
that you are still alive and here.

You are still here.

Still breathing in the quiet hours,
still standing through the fragile powers
of love that aches yet does not flee,
of loss that bends but does not break thee.

Love did not leave when voices ceased.
It only changed the way it speaks.
It walks beside you, slow and true,
in all the ways you carry through.

Some days it weighs upon your chest,
some days it softly lets you rest.
Some days it surprises you with light
you never planned to feel that night.

All of these days belong to you.
No pace to race, no proof is due.
You do not need to rush ahead
or live too far inside what's said.

Just stand where you are, as you have done,
with love not lost, but living on.

And when you close these pages now,
take this with you—quiet vow:
Nothing here was meant to mend,
or tie your grief to tidy ends.

It stayed with you when nights felt long,
until the room felt less than wrong.

And when you go—because you will—
through days uncertain, quiet, still,
you do not leave love far behind.

You carry it—
softly,
kind.

And that—
that is enough.

www.ingramcontent.com/pod-product-compliance
Lightning Source LLC
LaVergne TN
LVHW090531110826
845146LV00003B/1052

* 9 7 9 8 9 9 5 1 6 1 7 0 7 *